DON'T YOU DARE
HAVE KIDS
UNTIL YOU READ THIS!

Also by the author

DON'T YOU DARE GET MARRIED
UNTIL YOU READ THIS!

THE BOOK OF QUESTIONS FOR COUPLES

DON'T YOU DARE HAVE KIDS UNTIL YOU READ THIS!

THE BOOK OF QUESTIONS FOR PARENTS-TO-BE

COREY DONALDSON

THREE RIVERS PRESS

NEW YORK

Published by Three Rivers Press, New York, New York.
Member of the Crown Publishing Group,
a division of Random House, Inc.
www.randomhouse.com

THREE RIVERS PRESS and the Tugboat design are registered
trademarks of Random House, Inc.

Printed in the United States of America

Design by Lenny Henderson

Library of Congress Cataloging-in-Publication Data
Donaldson, Corey.
Don't you dare have kids until you read this!: a book of questions for
parents-to-be / Corey Donaldson.—1st ed.
1. Parenting.   I. Title.
HQ755.8 .D66   2003
649'.1—dc21   2002010958

ISBN 0-609-80912-1

10 9 8 7 6 5 4 3 2 1

First Edition

To My Firstborn
The Way Is Being Prepared for You.

Acknowledgments

This book is the result of so much input from many people!

I want my Mum and Dad to know that I am thankful for their example, for all they have done and all they will do. Thank you to all my ten brothers and sisters and the experiences they have shared. They are Glen (the Bear), Travis (T-Nips), Heath (H-Nips), Brooke (Bee-diddly), Kiran (Ears), Ryan (Jing-a-ling), Leigh (Cube), Craig (Baze), Abby (Yabo), and B.J. (the Bull). Thank you to Dale Dorning, my closest and most cherished friend, who has not only contributed greatly to this book but been a constant source of hope and encouragement. Thank you to my editor, Carrie Thornton, who has contributed greatly and has shown so much patience. Thank you to my agent, Brian DeFiore, for all he puts up with. He endures me well with his patience and keen insight.

Thank you also to David Shamy, Lorenzo Spencer,

ACKNOWLEDGMENTS

Terie Wiederhold, Michelle Fesolia, Monte Judd, Rob and Vickie Benincosa, Kevin Day, Ben and Jake Fullmer, Ginny Benincosa, little Madison, and Trudie.

Thank you to my dear wife, Phaidra, who has been more supportive of me than I could have dreamed. She is a wonderful person, and I have grown to love her more and more as each of the years of our great marriage pass by.

Contents

DON'T YOU DARE
HAVE KIDS
UNTIL YOU READ THIS!

WHY IS THIS BOOK NECESSARY?

One of the greatest things about shopping for food on a day when it's one hundred degrees outside is that moment when you walk through the doors of the supermarket and first feel that charge of icy air wrap around your entire body. From that moment on I look forward to a pleasurable shopping adventure, as my senses are tantalized with the crisp coolness of the air, the bright new colors of the seasonal fruits, and the seductive aroma of the freshly baked bread and pastries. It's no wonder I always spend more money than I plan to.

On one occasion like many others, my wife and I were shopping together in midafternoon. Phaidra began at the top of the shopping list she had diligently prepared, and I let my nose do the leading, which invariably led to feelings of guilt about things that should not have gone into the cart, and a reprimand from my wife as she patted my gut. My rationalizations about working out enough to compensate didn't hold water with Phaidra, but I tried to sway her by showering her with affection, telling her I loved her and how great she looked. I finally sealed the con with a tender kiss, hoping that this would take her mind off my indulgence.

As I stood in the middle of the aisle showing affection to Phaidra, out of nowhere came a little kid running at a hundred miles per hour. He dashed by and stepped on my foot. Hot on his trail was a vexed mother with blood visibly pumping through the veins in her forehead and neck, her steely eyes fixed on her prey. She was gaining on him, the back of her right hand poised to strike the kid into oblivion. I turned to Phaidra and said, "Yeah, we're having kids real soon."

My wife and I have had this conversation many times. We ask ourselves why we would want to exchange a relatively stress-free life for one filled with diapers, runny noses, public embarrassments, sleep deprivation, medical costs, worry, and the destruction of personal property and clothing, not to mention sprints down the supermarket aisle like a ferocious African wildcat after its victim. Why does anyone have children? Is it because everyone else does? Is there a religious motivation?

Maybe there are those who have never imagined not having children and look forward to the promise of some real or imagined measure of fulfillment.

I was raised as the second eldest of eleven children in Victoria, Australia. I cannot even begin to comprehend what raising us must have been like from my parents' perspective. What I can tell you is that my mother was and is an angel in human form. She was always available when I got home from school; she listened to my stories of the day and helped me with my homework. Mother was there to mend a broken heart and wipe away the blood from all the cuts and bruises that I seemed to get on a daily basis. She showed, then and now, the care and concern of a compassionate nurse and the tenderness and patience of . . . well, a loving parent. She fits the very definition of selflessness, having devoted her entire life to her children. While some mothers say, "I need my own life," my mother declared that we were her life. She gave and gave and still continues to give, for her evolved nature and great interest in ensuring a sense of humaneness in her little part of the world mean that she knows no way but unconditional devotion. If you need a measure to determine greatness in a mother, in a woman, she

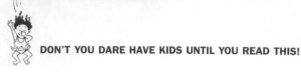

is it! In my mind, all great mothers must be compared to my Mum.

My father, in turn, was the breadwinner. He worked long hours, only to come home to misbehaving children that he had to discipline. We weren't always bad, but when we were it was his duty to mete out the punishment. Even so, he always hugged us and expressed love afterward. I respected that as I thought about it later in life. What my dad was telling me by doing this was that I had done something wrong and here was my punishment, but he loved me very much.

What stands out most about my father, though, was the affection he had for my Mum and for each of his children. He always wanted to spend more time with us than he could. When we went on vacations together as a family, we children were all thoroughly spoiled. I also remember the occasions when my dad spent time just with me, talking to me and listening to my concerns, hopes, and dreams. That meant a lot to me then, and it does now.

Even as I consider my own upbringing, I continually find myself asking the same questions about starting my own family. Do I want to go through the trials and hardships I saw my parents go through? Could it be that I focus too much on the difficult side of parenting and not the joyous side? Perhaps there is no negative side, just a side that forces you to grow. Am I getting closer to the truth? Could it be that what I am really facing is a resistance to growth and change? Do I want to exchange a world where everything is predictable for one in which I must surrender control? Am I just plain selfish? Maybe it's not my calling in life to be a parent—but how do I know?

There are other issues to consider beyond my own mind-set. Is the relationship my wife and I have secure enough to introduce parenthood into the mix? Is there a certain length of time a couple should be together before undertaking parenthood? What if a couple has been together too long—is there a danger that they will be too set in their ways to make room for a baby? Could it occur that I will want children before my wife does, or vice versa, and what happens then? There is so much to consider, it is difficult to know where to begin.

Don't get me wrong; I do see myself as a father. I know that when I hold my child for the first time, I will lift it high to present it to the heavens as I beam with a tender sense of emotion. I will reflect on my dad's best piece of parenting advice: "If you don't become a better man than I, I have failed as a father." When my dad said that, the burden of responsibility fell on his shoulders, and when I usher a child into this world that weight will be mine to bear. What an overwhelming sense of responsibility this presents.

The fact is, I am not prepared to rush into parenting just because my peers are doing it, or because my family and friends want me to. At the end of the day it is my wife and I who must raise our child, not those exerting outside pressure, as subtle as it may be. I am resolved that when the time comes I will be equipped for parenting in every way that a prospective parent can be equipped, and I say that with the understanding that nothing can prepare someone for parenting like parenting.

Yes, there is the fear of change and growth and the heartache that may come with being a parent, but it's so much more than that. Some of my hesitation comes from the knowledge that we will be entirely accountable for a pure and innocent child. Given that I am not a fan of surprises and that I take this mantle of parenting very seriously, I want to make sure that I consider all that needs to be considered before making the imperishable commitment of parenthood.

The next step, then, is to answer this question: How can I be prepared for parenthood in such a way that I do not repeat the mistakes of other parents and can also benefit from their triumphs? As I pose this question I think forward to the time when I will tell my own child, *If you don't become a better person than I, I have failed as a father.* What characteristics and resources can I offer my child to ensure that he or she does become a better person than I? Moreover, am I prepared for the day when my child begins to realize that I am a man prone to weakness, that I possess traits that are less than desirable or even unsavory?

Do you see what is happening here? The more I interrogate my own thoughts about parenthood and those of others, the more curious and inquiring I become. I can be confident about the prospect of becoming a father because of the questions I am prepared to confront. Questions are the difference between what we know and what we don't know about life. Anything worthwhile in life deserves to be explored through provocative questions that expose the unknown. Ignorance is no asset, nothing to be admired, especially when we elect to take on the nurturing of a soul who will, in the end, teach us more than we teach it. Yes—we learn from children. I know that when a child comes into the world, it comes a ready and competent tutor, which calls to mind the cliché "When the student is ready the teacher appears." So I come back to this point: What do I need to do to be a worthy and skilled pupil? I need to know the questions that must be faced that determine my willingness, not to mention worthiness, to be a parent!

I have always believed that the best advice and counsel come from those who have achieved what we desire. Alternatively, we can also benefit from noting the mistakes made by those who have led lives punctuated with regret and misery. The questions that I present in this book will come from accomplished parents, family therapy experts, media surveys, doctors, religious leaders, child care experts, and authors. It is my intention not only to expose the questions that will help to determine one's compatibility with parenthood, but to assist would-be parents in welcoming their infant and making parenthood compatible with their existing lifestyle.

My greatest hope, as I researched this book, was that

you and I would come to understand what it really takes to welcome and embrace this high and holy responsibility. It is my hope that as a result of reading this book, prospective parents and society as a whole will cease the ill-treatment of children altogether. I want parents who are not worthy of a child to not have one! When unprepared adults have children, they curse themselves, the child, and generations of children to come. I firmly believe that just because you can have children doesn't mean you should. My intention is not to pass judgment on who is or is not a good parent, but to unearth the actions and attitudes that can indicate questionable priorities and perhaps the inability to raise healthy children. The purpose here is not only to make us aware of any wrong actions that may seem innocent to us, but also to make us aware of how these actions can affect children. It is my feeling that if certain questions are confronted, as outlined in this book, we will see errors in our judgment and flaws in our character that require attention. Then, if we are diligent, we'll make the appropriate adjustments to our behavior to ensure that we can give a child an upbringing to be cherished.

Our society must deal with children who have been

molested, malnourished, emotionally and physically abused, and witnesses to the poor example of parents who abuse their own bodies through the use of addictive and mind-altering substances. I have been repulsed by parents who freely smoke in a closed environment, giving an infant no other choice but to breathe the carcinogenic fumes into its delicate lungs. I have seen homes where pornography is readily available on the coffee table. This is not an environment for children! People with such tendencies have questionable parenting abilities, in my opinion. At the very least, I hope that reading this book may stir up enough apprehension about parenthood in such people that they abstain from it. Again, I am not saying that such people are necessarily bad; rather, they engage in activities that do not promote the well-being of children, and therefore they may not be fit for parenthood.

There have been many times I have thought that the government should require would-be parents to be licensed to have children. You need a license to get married, to drive a car, to run a business—why not to have a child? Is a child not more important?

When my wife and I see children who live under cir-

cumstances such as those described above, we sometimes feel that we should take care of such children
ourselves. We feel very deeply that with our combined
talents, the atmosphere of our home would be a fine
place for a child to be raised—we feel that we have so
much to offer. With this in mind, one of the greatest
purposes of this book is to serve those who already know
they have so much to offer a child. For those of us in this
category, we desire to make a difference and refine our
parenting skills. The questions posed in this book will
help us to that end.

Surely there are more questions to consider than are
contained in this book. Nevertheless, the ones noted
here will help you determine your mental state when it
comes to your motivation for having children. You will
be able to examine your willingness to teach and, moreover, be taught. What I look forward to most is making
a difference in my child's life. I hope that someday my
child will be able to reflect on me and say, "My father has
prepared me to be a better person than he is; now I must
do the same for my children."

HOW I CAME TO WRITE THIS BOOK

I n my first book, *Don't You Dare Get Married Until You Read This,* I identified more than five hundred questions in eleven categories that couples should consider before they get married. The questions in that book were based on interviews with over fifteen hundred people over a four-year period. The purpose of that book is to help couples make more intelligent marriage decisions so that they will not fall prey to divorce. Essentially, my first book is about anticipating difficult issues before marriage so that couples have a chance to address them before they say "I do."

Of course, the natural step after marriage is having children, and so a whole new set of questions has to be considered. Hence this book, with questions that are just as relevant, just as poignant, perhaps even just as threatening as the ones to be considered before marriage.

The questions in this book are based on interviews I

gave to the media, and the articles these journalists wrote asking their readers to submit questions. I have consulted once again with family, friends and professionals. I have read many family and parenting books and was able to create questions based on my interpretations. I also had many questions left over from the research I did for my first book that fit better here.

As I was writing this book and speaking about it incessantly with many patient people, two questions arose more than once: *What right do you have to write a book on the questions to ask before you have children? You have no children of your own—what do you know?* These questions are most intriguing and are worthy of a response here.

I began compiling questions for my first book before I got married because at the time I could not find a book that would tell me the questions I should consider before tying the knot. Since there was no such book, I began to ask people their advice—and if you have read my first book, you will see how great their advice was. I now have a very happy marriage.

The reason I was seeking these questions at that particular time was that it had occurred to me that marriage is something to be prepared for before you do it, not after. I felt that if I could learn from others' experiences, I would not have to repeat their mistakes. Why on earth would I want to get married, fail at it, *then* learn about what not to do? This is a bizarre notion.

Why should it be any different with becoming a parent? Should I begin to learn how to become a good parent before the child comes, or wait until the child arrives to begin to take notice? It is all a matter of timing. If you are going to be a parent, you will learn about it at some point. Most people start learning about parenting when they realize they are pregnant and know nothing. I just want to be prepared before reality hits, not after.

I know that regardless of what I know and what I learn, I will be an imperfect parent, but surely it is true that I can stack the odds in my favor by increasing my knowledge. Asking questions before parenthood is about substituting awareness for ignorance. Do I already have to be a parent to want awareness? Of course not!

HOW TO USE THIS BOOK

This book can be studied by an individual, particularly the chapter titled "Are You Ready to Be a Parent?" Nevertheless, it would be wise to study this book as a couple. Studying the questions together will reveal much about each partner that you did not already know. You will come to comprehend each other's parenting style before you are parents. You will see how each would react to difficult issues, and you can begin to unearth areas of disagreement and conflict you may have. Perhaps most important, you will come to see a side of yourself that you did not know existed. You may not even know what type of parent you will be until you face these questions—in short, you will reveal yourself to yourself.

My wife and I have begun asking these questions of each other as we contemplate becoming parents. One of the interesting discoveries that came about as we disagreed on certain points of view was that we could see how disagreements could occur in front of the children. This realization caused us to ask how we will handle such disagreements. We came to agree on an answer to this question, but we also realized that answering any other question in the book can reveal more questions. I therefore encourage couples who read this book together to look beyond what is here for other issues that may surface.

Please don't believe that you are meant to feel like you'll be a perfect parent after you have considered all the questions. This is about determining what you do know and do not know, about assessing your attitude toward parenting as an individual and as a couple. Armed with this knowledge, you will be better equipped to reinforce your strengths and to make your weaknesses fade as much as possible.

Are You Ready to Be a Parent?

1. Why do you want children?

2. What are you not prepared to sacrifice when you become a parent?

3. Just because you can have children, does that mean you should?

4. What do you fear most about being a parent?

5. What makes you think you are worthy to have a child?

6. What makes you unworthy to have children?

7. How many parents do you know who are really happy being a parent? What does that tell you?

8. To what extent do you surrender control of your life when you become a parent?

9. When someone decides to be a parent, does that person become a teacher or a student?

10. What do you need to change about yourself before you have children?

11. What are you doing in your life right now that you would not want your child to do? What will it take for you to stop that action right now?

12. How important do you think it is for children to hear "I'm sorry" or "I was wrong" from their parents? Why or why not?

The Top Ten Things Not *to Say When Your Wife Announces She Is Pregnant*

10. *You'd better not get fat!*
 9. *Just don't ask me to get out of bed in the middle of the night!*
 8. *Don't expect me to put up with any whining!*
 7. *Yeah, but where's dinner?*
 6. *Are you sure?*
 5. *What are you going to do?*
 4. *It had better not be a girl!*
 3. *Who's the father?*
 2. *Can't you see I'm busy?*
 1. *Shh,* The Simpsons *is on!*

COREY DONALDSON

13. If your child could see the way you treat the people in your life right now, what would your child learn?

14. What do children learn from you when they hear you talk about others negatively?

15. To what extent will your children learn honesty and integrity from what you do rather than what you say?

16. To what extent do you want your child to achieve things you did not achieve?

17. If it is true that life's greatest lessons come from our greatest challenges, do you think that being a parent will be your greatest challenge? What lessons do think you will learn from your children?

18. What type of child do you need to become a person of sound wisdom?

19. Which of your past sins or imperfections do you not want your children to know about? Why?

20. Can you financially afford to have children?

21. How do you expect your lifestyle to change when children come?

22. Which aspects of your lifestyle are you not prepared to change after you have children?

Attention Parents

All calamities and all suffering . . . are sent to us out of mercy to help us evolve and find our true selves. . . . People who are tested are fortunate, but when you find your true self, suffering is no longer necessary. And not only is it no longer necessary, it is no longer possible.

MARK FISHER,
THE MILLIONAIRE'S SECRETS

23. To what extent are children to be seen and not heard?

24. To what extent do you want your child to take an interest in your hobbies or activities?

25. What would it mean to you if your child took zero interest in your activities or hobbies?

26. Would you want to be raised by you?

27. How do you know if you are worthy to have children?

28. Would you consider hiring help to assist with the housework and yard work?

29. Why is it important to you to know that your children are proud of what you do?

30. How will you make your children proud of you?

31. How do you feel about reading how-to books on child rearing?

32. How possible is it that your work or a hobby could constantly take you away from the family? How will you compensate if it does?

33. Do you think it is wrong to favor one child's personality over another's? Why?

34. What does it take in terms of personal character to be a full-time mom or dad?

The way you treat any relationship in the family will eventually affect every relationship in the family.

STEPHEN COVEY

Anyone with preschool children should be compelled to leave the workplace by 5:30 P.M.—this means dads, too.

KAY WILLS

"Oh God, are you home from school already?"

MOTHER OF THREE

One of the best things a man can do for his children is love their mother.

FATHER THEODORE HESBURGH

When she calls me on the cell phone and asks me how far I am from home, I know things are really bad.

FATHER OF FOUR

[*All of the five preceding excerpts are from:* Are We Having Fun Yet? The Sixteen Secrets of Happy Parenting, *by Kay Willis and Maryanne Bucknum Brinley.*]

A Job Description for Mothers

Wanted: Athlete in top condition to safeguard tireless toddler. Needs quick reflexes, boundless energy, infinite patience. ESP helpful, knowledge of first aid essential. Must be able to drive, cook, phone, work despite constant distractions. Workday: fifteen hours. Will consider pediatric nurse with Olympic background. Training in psychology desirable. Should be able to referee and must be unflappable. Tolerance is chief requirement.

JOAN BECK, NEWSPAPER COLUMNIST

35. How much selfishness are you willing to give up to be a parent?

36. If you were to have a mission statement for what you want to accomplish as a father or mother, how would it read?

37. Which of these two attitudes will you most likely adopt as a parent: "I didn't have it, so you won't have it" or "I didn't have it, so you will have it"?

38. Would you consider baby-sitting an infant or child for an extended time to determine if parenting is for you?

39. Would you use a doll that mimics the behavior of a real baby to determine your compatibility with parenthood?

40. Is quality parenting more an issue of intuition or of acquired knowledge?

41. To what extent is there a correlation between being an effective parent and being physically fit?

42. How will you teach your children not to repeat your mistakes and those of humanity?

43. What will you teach your children about the value of adversity?

Every child is an artist. The problem is how to remain an artist once he grows up.

PABLO PICASSO

When we listen as if we were in a temple and give our attention to one another as if each person were our teacher, honoring his or her words as valuable and sacred, all kinds of great possibilities awaken. Even miracles can happen.

JACK KORNFIELD, *A PATH WITH HEART*

44. How will you teach your son or daughter about the effects of selfishness?

45. What efforts will you make to ensure that you are a parent who does what you say?

46. Is it important to you that your children consider you to be their hero?

47. How must you live to be considered your child's hero?

48. Which words do you currently use that you will not tolerate from your children?

49. If you are an immigrant or your parents were, how important is it to you that your children be knowledgeable about the history of your or your parents' native country?

50. How important will it be to you to share the experiences of your childhood with your children?

51. What do you think it will mean to your children to know about your experiences as a child?

52. Are great relationships with children a matter of luck or the result of attention and effort?

53. Is a parent's role to teach his or her children *what* to think or *how* to think?

54. What influences in your life will play the greatest role as you consider raising a child?

When two people fight and shout at each other,
they are both sending messages but neither is
receiving, so discommunication takes place.

BRENTON G. YORGASON,
FROM FIRST DATE TO CHOSEN MATE

55. What uncertainties come with parenthood?

56. If you could talk to your child as an adult right now, what would be his or her biggest complaint about you?

57. Have you ever felt the inclination to harm children in any way? Have you acted on it?

58. Have you ever been sexually molested?

59. Does a person who has been molested have to fight inclinations to molest others?

60. In what ways does having been molested make a person a better or worse parent?

61. What kind of parent would you be if your spouse died after the birth of your child?

62. Have you ever caught yourself thinking that having children is necessary so that you will be taken care of in your old age?

63. What does it mean, exactly, to be "taken care of" during old age?

64. How wise is it to expect your children to care for you when you are old?

65. To what extent is it wrong to want children because your peers are having children?

66. To what extent could it be good training for parenthood to raise dogs or cats?

People have innate impulses to get married and become parents, but there is no in-built program for how to do either.

Where people get stuck in parenting is an indication of where they are stunted psychologically.

The process of becoming a conscious marriage partner is similar to the process of becoming a conscious parent.

HARVILLE HENDRIX AND HELEN HUNT,
GIVING THE LOVE THAT HEALS

67. If your child constantly talks and makes noise everywhere in the house, would that annoy you? What would you do about it?

68. How long could you withstand incessant talking/crying/singing/complaining by your toddler in the backseat while you are driving?

69. What have you learned about yourself as a result of considering these questions thus far?

Is Your Marriage Ready for a Child?

1. What makes your marriage stable enough to introduce children into the mix?

2. Why should you not have children?

3. What is more important, your relationship with your children or that with your spouse? Why?

4. Which, if any, of the duties of caring for an infant do you consider to be man's or woman's work?

5. Is it possible that a motivation for one or both of you to have children is that you think it will save your dying relationship? What precedents are there that this actually works positively?

6. Which are the responsibilities of parenthood that only a father or mother should fulfill?

7. What is it about your spouse that you trust when it comes to parenting?

8. What is it about your spouse that you do not trust when it comes to parenting?

9. If your spouse makes a mistake in judgment or behavior, what efforts will you make not to humiliate or correct him or her in front of the children?

10. To what extent is it true that if children do not turn out to be better people than the parents, then the parents have failed?

Better build schoolrooms for "the boy"
Than cells and gibbets for "the man"

ELIZA COOK,
A SONG FOR THE RAGGED SCHOOLS

I now have a great relationship with my father
and have forgiven him, but I will never forget the
pain of being invisible. I wouldn't have minded it
if he had just looked up and said, "I'm busy—I'll
talk to you later." But to be invisible!

ELLEN GALINSKY,
ASK THE CHILDREN

11. What constitutes success as a parent?

12. What constitutes failure as a parent?

13. What would your life be like if you were never to have children at all?

14. How often will just the two of you go on a date after you have children?

15. What are your thoughts about how you and your spouse should handle marital disagreements when they occur in the children's presence?

16. How prepared are you for the possibility that your child could be born with a mental or physical disability?

17. What effect will having children have on your relationship with your spouse?

18. Should couples who are not getting along stay together for the children?

19. How would you feel about being a parent if you and your spouse were not happy together?

20. Are there any specific activities that only the father or mother should be involved in with a child? If so, what are they?

21. What strengths does a married couple bring into a child's life, as opposed to a couple that lives together but is not married?

It's the way parents interact with their children, rather than how kids see their parents behave towards one another, that has the biggest impact on how children learn to behave in their own adult relationships.

RAND CONGER IN *WORKING MOTHER*, MAY 2001

If you're like most parents, you'd like to shield your children from rejection. You can't. Rejection is a part of every child's life. And no matter how hard you try to make your child's life comfortable and secure, he's still going to have to live life with some rejection.

DEBORA PHILLIPS,
HOW TO GIVE YOUR CHILD A GREAT SELF-IMAGE

22. What level of affection is appropriate or inappropriate in front of the children?

23. What is good about children seeing their mother and father being affectionate with each other?

24. Which aspects of your spouse's character and disposition do you think need the most change in order for your spouse to be the best parent he or she can be?

25. What is it about your spouse that makes you glad she or he will be a parent to your child?

26. What makes you think that your marriage is stable enough to raise an emotionally well-adjusted child?

27. How much truth is there to the notion that one purpose of being a parent is to prepare your children for marriage?

28. Who will pick up after the children if they don't do so themselves?

29. What does it mean when couples say they have to put their marriage on hold while they raise the children?

30. Should a mother never work outside the home after having children?

Not all people are lovable, but when we find someone difficult for us to love, it is often because they remind us of something within ourselves that we do not like.

BETTY J. EADIE, *EMBRACED BY THE LIGHT*

Each of us is 100 percent responsible for the relationships we create.

TAYLOR HARTMAN, *THE COLOR CODE*

If there is any one secret of success, it lies in the ability to get the other person's point of view and see things from his angle as well as from your own.

HENRY FORD

31. What name will you give your child if it is a boy or a girl?

32. If your last names are different, which name will your child have?

33. What will be your child's middle name?

34. What adjustments in attitude and in lifestyle will you need to make if you have twins?

35. How far into pregnancy will you continue to make love?

36. How long will you wait to make love after the child is born?

37. How many children do you want to have?

38. How much time should pass before having another child?

39. Does one parent bear more responsibility for raising the child than the other?

40. In what ways are your roles as parents different but equal?

41. How will you decide who gets up in the middle of the night when the baby needs tending?

42. What are the issues unique to your relationship that you need to consider in conjunction with parenthood?

Humans do not bloom in environments where creativity is crushed and where memorizing facts, figures and formulas that adults deem necessary take priority.

Until our educational system stops punishing and ignoring people for making mistakes and until the creation of money is made part of the school curriculum, people will continue to live lives as codependent wimps who only know how to ask, "Where is my paycheck?"

ROBERT KIYOSAKI, *IF YOU WANT TO BE RICH AND HAPPY, DON'T GO TO SCHOOL*

43. What would you do if one of you decides not to have children after you get married, when you had both agreed beforehand that you would have children?

44. What would it take for you to attend a support group for parents who are having difficulty with parenthood?

45. What is the greatest source of conflict between you and your spouse regarding parenting ideas?

46. Could this area of conflict cause a divorce?

47. What will you do to ensure that this area of conflict does not cause a divorce after the children arrive?

48. What effects do you think divorce has on children?

49. How would it affect you if after your first child your spouse had less or no desire for sex?

50. Do you expect that after childbirth your sexual activity will be the same as before?

51. Is it unreasonable to expect the same sexual activity after having given birth?

52. If your future children could see the way you and your spouse treat each other right now, what

And whoso shall receive one such little child in my name receiveth me. But whoso shall offend one of these little ones which believe in me, it were better for him that a millstone were hanged about his neck, and that he were drowned in the depth of the sea.

MATTHEW 18:5–6

would they learn about how to have a successful marriage?

53. What efforts will you make not to disagree in front of the children about your views on discipline?

54. If you grew up in a single-parent home, will that influence you to believe the entire parenting responsibility is yours alone?

55. If your upbringing makes you feel that parenting is solely your responsibility, do you think that could alienate your spouse? What could this alienation lead to?

56. Do you think that those raised in a single-parent home subconsciously re-create this dynamic even if they are married?

57. Are you emotionally mature?

58. Is emotional maturity a prerequisite for becoming a good parent? Why?

59. Should parents teach children how to be emotionally mature, or is that the task of the larger world?

60. How can emotional maturity be taught?

61. Which meals of the day will you eat as a family?

62. If you brought your infant to your bed and he or

Man is not the creature of circumstances.
Circumstances are the creatures of men.

BENJAMIN DISRAELI

It is essential that a child have the experience of
failure to learn that it is okay to make mistakes.

JOHN GRAY, *HOW TO GET WHAT YOU WANT*
AND WANT WHAT YOU HAVE

If we are not intimate with our emotions, we
cannot perceive the dynamics that lie behind
emotions, the ways these dynamics work, and the
ends that they serve.

GARY ZUKAV, *THE SEAT OF THE SOUL*

she was very fussy, how would you feel if your spouse left to sleep in another room?

63. If you are female, how would your spouse react if you became pregnant by accident?

64. How would you feel if, after your spouse got home from work at the end of the day to find the house a mess, he or she said, "What have you been doing all day?"

65. What are the chances that all the answers you give to the above questions will fly out the window once the baby arrives?

Pregnancy and Childbirth

1. If you are male, what are you not prepared to sacrifice during the pregnancy?

2. What lifestyle change will each of you need to make during pregnancy?

3. Are you likely to resent having to make any of those lifestyle changes?

4. What would you do if you had to sell your car to cut expenses in order to have a child?

5. What would you do if you had to sell your house to cut expenses in order to have a child?

6. Do you think that you need to be living in a house (as opposed to an apartment or a condo) before you get pregnant? Why?

7. How will you have to adjust your budget during the pregnancy? After the child is born?

8. Is your health insurance adequate to cover the expenses for mother and child, even if complications occur?

9. What does your health insurance not cover during pregnancy and childbirth?

10. If you are male, are you prepared to make late-night runs to the grocery store to satisfy your pregnant wife's food cravings, to care for her

If you are prepared for disappointment, you have a chance of turning that disappointment into an asset. Most turn disappointment into a liability—a long-term one.

An upset is our maker's way of telling us that we need to learn something. . . . If you lie, blame, justify, or deny the upset, you waste the upset and will waste a precious gem of wisdom.

People come together to teach each other lessons.

ROBERT KIYOSAKI,
RICH DAD, POOR DAD SERIES

when she's feeling tired or nauseated, and to patiently respond to any manner of emotional outbursts and irrational behavior during the pregnancy?

11. Will you go together to the doctor's office during and after pregnancy?

12. Whom do you want or not want in the room during the actual birth?

13. Who will be the first people you call to tell of the birth of your child?

14. If you already have children, would you want them in the room to witness the birth of their brother or sister?

15. What are the pros and cons of your own children witnessing the birth of their new brother or sister?

16. Do you want to give birth at a hospital or at home?

17. Should you videotape the birth of your child?

18. If a husband can hear his wife vomiting from nausea early in the morning or in the middle of the night, does he have the right to ask her to close the door?

*Children growing up in violent homes evidence
many of the same symptoms as children growing
up in alcoholic homes . . . emotional triangulations,
secrets and isolation, stressed relationships, failing
finances and hopelessness.*

RICHARD GELLES AND DONILEEN LOSEKE,
CURRENT CONTROVERSIES ON FAMILY VIOLENCE

19. How will the responsibility for household chores and duties change during the pregnancy?

20. If you are male, how would your feelings toward your wife change if she gained a lot of weight during pregnancy and did not lose it afterward?

21. How will you determine which doctor you want to use in the birth of your child?

22. Does it make a difference to you whether the obstetrician is male or female?

23. At what point do you wish to know the sex of your child—when your doctor knows or at birth?

24. If you are male, how do you think you would respond if your wife became very sick during or after pregnancy?

25. Would you want any tests done on your unborn baby to see if there are any genetic defects?

26. If you learned early in the pregnancy that your child would be born physically or mentally challenged, what would you do? How would you feel?

27. For how long would you keep your newborn baby on life support if needed and if there were no sign of recovery?

28. Is there an age after which women should, for

In the families with suicidal teenagers, that child was constantly ignored and put down in conversations.

KATHLEEN MCCOY,
COPING WITH TEENAGE DEPRESSION

medical reasons, definitely stop trying to have children?

29. What effect is there on an unborn baby if the mother smokes, or if she is exposed to secondhand smoke?

30. Whom will you go to for advice when things come up during the pregnancy that you are unsure about?

31. Who is more qualified to give correct pregnancy advice, the wife's mother or the husband's?

32. How do you think you would cope with a miscarriage?

33. If you had a miscarriage, how long would you want to wait before trying to have another child?

34. What are the pros and cons of learning about all the things that can go wrong during and after pregnancy?

35. If the child is a boy, should he be circumcised?

36. How old is too old to begin having children?

Child Care

1. Who will take the children to activities after school and on the weekends?

2. What limits, if any, should you place on your children's activities to ensure that you and your spouse each have time to enjoy your own activities and interests?

3. How much will the "tooth fairy" give your children for each lost tooth? Will you even allow this tradition?

4. Is each of you willing to change the infant's diapers, bathe the baby, feed and dress the child? How often?

5. If you to use day care, which type will you use— family, friends, or public or private facilities?

6. How will you pay for the baby's clothes, food, medical care, and other needs?

7. What are the positive and negative aspects of having a family dog or cat around new babies or small children?

8. If the father is the sole breadwinner, does that mean the sole responsibility of caring for a crying baby at night is the mother's?

9. How do you feel about piercing an infant's ears?

No man with a trace of horse sense would expect a child of three years old to react to the viewpoint of a father thirty years old.

DALE CARNEGIE,

HOW TO WIN FRIENDS AND INFLUENCE PEOPLE

10. Whom do you want never to baby-sit your children?

11. Is there anyone who would make you feel uneasy if that person were left alone with your infant or child?

12. What types of food should infants eat?

13. Do you know the most common sicknesses new babies have, the symptoms of each, and how to treat them?

14. How long does a baby need to cry before you should take it to the doctor?

15. Is it necessary to pick the baby up every time it cries? Why?

16. What efforts will you make to babyproof your home?

17. At what age will you begin to toilet-train your child?

18. How do you toilet-train a child?

19. If your child is calmed by riding in the car, would you drive for hours on end to keep the child quiet?

20. How do you feel about placing the infant safely in another room of the house to get away from the crying?

You must never take the baby out of the car seat while the car is moving. No matter how desperate she is to be picked up. A child is never safe in her mother's arms while the car is moving no matter how careful and protective you might feel.

VICKY IOVINE

How sharper than a serpent's tooth it is to have a thankless child.

SHAKESPEARE,
KING LEAR

21. How old should an infant be before he or she gets a bath for the first time?

22. Will you read to your child? How often? Who will do it?

23. Will you play music for your child? What kind?

24. How often will you give your child candy or dessert?

25. What efforts will you make to ensure that your child is physically active?

26. At what age should you give your children multi-vitamins, if at all?

27. Will you take your children to a salon to have a haircut, or will you learn to do it yourself to save money?

28. Do you think you have to provide entertainment every minute of the day for young children?

29. At what age does a child become too old to sleep with Mom and Dad?

30. At what age is it appropriate for a child to have a swing set in the backyard?

31. When should a child start walking?

32. Should you invest in a video camera so that you can capture the early days of your youngster's life?

I was carrying my one-year-old daughter, Riplee, along the side of the road when we came to a low tree branch. I told her, "The tree is going to hit your head. Duck." She responded instinctively, "Quack, quack."

JENNIFER BURKART IN *PARENTS*, MAY 2001

Children begin by loving their parents; as they grow older they judge them; sometimes they forgive them.

OSCAR WILDE,
THE PICTURE OF DORIAN GRAY

All bachelors love dogs, and we would love children
just as much if they would be taught to retrieve.

P. J. O'ROURKE,
THE BACHELOR HOME COMPANION

33. How often should Mom, Dad, or both take time off from work, household chores, and their own interests just to play with their child?

34. Should time spent with children happen randomly, or by deliberate appointment?

35. When you change diapers, will you do it barehanded or wear protective gloves?

36. How do you know when it is safe for a child to eat solid food?

37. Do you think it is acceptable for an infant or child to drink carbonated beverages?

38. How often does an infant need to be bathed?

39. Do you believe your child should receive immunizations?

40. At what age should the following immunization shots be administered: hepatitis B, DTP, hemophilus B, polio (IPV or OPV), varicella, MMR?

41. Should an infant sleep on its back or its stomach?

42. If your child screams when you take him or her to preschool for the first time, will you leave or stay? What if it happens every time?

43. Are you aware of the symptoms a child exhibits when he or she has been molested?

The Toddler's Creed

If I want it, it's mine.

If I give it to you and change my mind later, it's mine.

If I can take it away from you, it's mine.

If it's mine, it will never belong to anybody else, no matter what.

If we are building something together, all the pieces are mine.

If it just looks like mine, it's mine.

UNKNOWN

44. At what age do you think a child begins learning the temperament of the others in the home?

45. How much should you pay to have a baby-sitter watch your child for the evening?

46. At what age should you begin having birthday parties to which children of the same age are invited?

47. Should you buy gifts for infants at birthdays or Christmas even though they have no idea what is going on?

48. How will you explain nightmares to a small child?

49. Do you think there is a relationship between excessive juice consumption and obesity in children?

50. Is optimism in a child inherited or learned?

51. How long should you wait before picking up your toddler's toys?

52. When you pick up your toddler's toys, should they be placed where the child can get to them again easily, or should they be hidden away?

53. Do both you and your spouse know how to change a diaper?

54. Should you change a diaper if only urine is in it?

55. Will you use cloth or disposable diapers?

When you've seen a nude infant doing a backward somersault you know why clothing exists.

STEPHEN FRY, *PAPERWEIGHT*

To my daughter Leonora, without whose never failing sympathy and encouragement this book would have been finished in half the time.

P. G. WODEHOUSE, DEDICATION TO *HEART OF A GOOF*

56. How long should it take for a child to learn how to go to the toilet alone?

57. At what age should a child have stopped wetting the bed ?

58. What should you do if your child continues to wet the bed beyond the normal period of time?

59. Will your child be breast- or bottle-fed?

60. Are you good examples for your children in terms of eating healthily?

61. How would you feel if another woman breast-fed your baby?

62. Do you know how to induce vomiting in case your child swallows poison?

63. At what age should a child first be taken to the dentist?

64. How often will you take your children to the dentist?

65. Once your children can bathe themselves, how often will you ask them to do it and at what time of day?

66. How do you tell the difference between the crying of an infant who is in pain and the tears of a baby who is crying for attention?

To laugh often and much; to win the respect of intelligent people and the affection of children; to earn the appreciation of honest critics and endure the betrayal of false friends; to appreciate beauty, to find the best in others; to leave the world a bit better, whether by a healthy child, a garden patch or a redeemed social condition; to know even one life has breathed easier because you have lived. This is to have succeeded.

RALPH WALDO EMERSON

67. How do you choose the right doctor for your child?

68. What do you do if your infant or child is stung by a bee?

69. How do you resuscitate an infant or child who has fallen into a pool and is not breathing?

70. How do you discover if your child has allergic reactions, before they occur?

71. Is there a shampoo that really will not sting your child's eyes?

72. What medical supplies should you always keep on hand for your child?

73. Why do you think that children need hugs from both Mom and Dad all through their lives?

74. At what age will you teach your children to swim?

75. How will you teach your children manners?

76. At what point will you develop and teach the home fire drill?

Disciplining Your Children

1. If you and your spouse have a major disagreement concerning discipline before you have children, should you just not have children at all?

2. What value is there in allowing your children to choose their own consequences for disobedience ahead of time?

3. If to discipline is to teach, what is the best method of discipline?

4. How ready are you to have your patience stretched to the limit by your children?

5. What will you do when your child answers you back with rudeness or displays flagrant disrespect?

6. If one of your children has wronged another of your children, should you allow revenge to take place without your involvement?

7. What is it about managing your own children that you want to experience?

8. How will you raise your children differently from the way you were raised?

9. What are the discipline strategies your parents used on you that were effective?

10. What were the discipline strategies your parents used that you did not respond well to?

Desire not a multitude of unprofitable children,
neither delight on ungodly sons.

ECCLESIASTES 16:1

11. What do you dislike about the way other parents discipline their children?

12. How do you feel about physical discipline as a means of punishment?

13. At what age should physical discipline begin?

14. How old is too old for a child to be spanked?

15. What would you do if your child hit you back after you spanked him or her?

16. At what point does spanking or hitting become child abuse?

17. How would you tutor your baby-sitter on the methods of discipline he or she is authorized use, or not to use?

18. Is it ever appropriate or effective to quote a biblical commandment as an attempt to enforce discipline, such as "Honor thy father and thy mother"?

19. If all your children were upset and crying at once, would you try to help the situation or would you leave the house to get away from the noise?

20. As you and your spouse work together to establish discipline policies for your children, how do you determine what is right rather than who is right?

21. To what extent should a parent become knowl-

Sometimes when I look at my children I say to myself, "Lillian, you should have stayed a virgin."

LILLIAN CARTER, MOTHER OF
PRESIDENT JIMMY CARTER

The business of being a child interests a child not at all. Children very rarely play at being other children.

DAVID HOLLOWAY, *DAILY TELEGRAPH*, 1966

edgeable in at least the elementary strategies of child counseling and psychotherapy?

22. At what time should children go to bed when they are in preschool, elementary school, junior high, and high school?

23. What kind of imperfections do you think will be revealed about yourself as you discipline your children?

24. When shopping for school clothes, will your children be given a predetermined spending limit, or will it be open season?

25. Will you be able to communicate just as effectively with your son as with your daughter, or vice versa?

26. What mistakes have you made in life that you do not want your children to make?

27. To avoid having your children repeat your mistakes, should you avoid telling your children exactly what your mistakes were?

28. If you child destroyed your $1,500 video camera, how do you discipline the child while at the same time communicating the message that he or she is more valuable to you than the camera?

The anticipation during the months of pregnancy is wonderful, but after you see your baby's face and feel his soft skin . . . once you hold that little infant in your arms . . . it becomes the dearest thing in your life.

AHMAD SHARIFI, *A SQUARE SKY*

29. Should children have the impression that you think you are always right?

30. How important is it to admit to your child when you are wrong?

31. If you are wrong, can you admit it to your child?

32. When the time comes that your parental instinct causes you to correct your child's misbehavior, what could be the advantage of showing your love for the child afterward with words of affection and a hug?

33. How would you respond if your child cursed at you?

34. Which words will you not tolerate your child using?

35. Would you discipline your child in front of guests or strangers, or wait for a private moment?

36. If a child's punishment involved forfeiting an outing or date, how would you make sure you did not cave in to the child's pleas by withdrawing the punishment?

37. What does a child learn when a parent does not carry out the discipline that was promised?

38. Is there a difference between willful disobedience in children or teens and simple irresponsibility?

39. How important is it to you that your children think of you as always in charge?

40. How effective do you think it would be to give your teen a curfew and tell him or her where not to go? Alternatively, how effective do you think it would be to tell your teen that you trust his or her judgment?

41. If your child is demonstrating prolonged behavioral problems, at what point does drug therapy become an option, if at all?

42. What would have to occur for you to seek professional help with your child's behavior?

43. If one of your children is upset at you and refuses to eat at the dinner table, would you allow the child to eat dinner in his or her room?

44. What value is there in asking your children their opinions on the rules in the home?

45. Would you treat your own biological child differently from an adopted child?

46. What control will you have over your children's use of the Internet?

47. How will you train your children to pick up after themselves?

48. How effective is the argument "As long as you're living in my house you will live under my rules"?

Difficult Parenting Issues

1. Who will be the breadwinner when you have children?

2. If you need to move for employment reasons but your children don't want to move, what impact, if any, will this have on your final decision?

3. How would you feel about your child marrying a person of another race?

4. How would you react if your child told you he or she was gay?

5. How would you treat your child differently if he or she were gay?

6. How would you feel if your gay son or daughter wanted to have a gay marriage?

7. Is there any scenario for which you would consider an abortion?

8. In considering the location for a family vacation, would the biggest influence be the interests of the children or your own interests?

9. What is the appropriate amount of money to spend on children at Christmas and on birthdays?

10. How do you feel about adopting a child instead of having your own?

11. Is the age of a prospective adopted child relevant?

Research has shown that the most effective way to reduce problem behavior in children is to strengthen desirable behavior through positive reinforcement rather than trying to weaken undesirable behavior using aversive or negative processes.

DR. SIDNEY W. BIJOU,
THE INTERNATIONAL ENCYCLOPEDIA
OF EDUCATION, 1998

12. How do you feel about adopting a child of a different race?

13. What do you need to consider when adopting a child who has been physically or mentally abused?

14. Does it matter what your existing children think when you are considering adoption?

15. If you adopted and the birth mother eventually wanted to reconnect, how would you react?

16. How would you feel about your adopted child wanting to seek out his or her birth parents?

17. How early would you tell a child that he or she was adopted?

18. How would you tell a child that he or she was adopted?

19. What would be the result of not telling your child about the adoption until he or she was a teenager?

20. Would you consider becoming a foster parent?

21. To what extent, if any, should the children be made aware of the financial concerns of the parents?

22. If your adult child were having a hard time getting a date, would you encourage him or her to take out a personal ad?

The first half of our lives is controlled by our parents. The second half is controlled by our children.

AUTHOR UNKNOWN

23. Do you think you are entitled to know everything about the life of your married child?

24. Would you consider having children by cloning yourself?

25. If it were possible, would you have a "designer kid" by scientifically eliminating the possibilities of imperfection and ensuring the presence of certain traits?

26. Is genetic engineering for straight teeth, intelligence, muscularity, and so on okay with you?

27. To what extent do you think children suffer academically at school during and after the divorce of their parents?

28. Do you believe parents should be involved in the marital problems of their children?

29. If parents get involved in the marital problems of their children, should they wait to be invited to do so or just invite themselves?

30. To what extent are the financial affairs of married children the business of parents?

31. What financial preparations do you need to make to ensure that your children can always participate in activities such as camp, excursions, sports, and higher education?

Misbehavior of children must be recognized as a need to teach appropriate behavior, not as an excuse to punish. Punishment is a terrible teacher; it only teaches children how not to behave.

DR. GLENN LATHAM,
THE POWER OF POSITIVE PARENTING

32. If you do not have insurance and your child is injured while in the care of a baby-sitter, who should be responsible for the bill?

33. Would you seek professional help if you suffered from postpartum depression?

34. What does it mean if your child creates imaginary friends?

35. Whose Christmas (or other holiday) traditions will you follow—those of the wife's family or those of the husband's?

36. What do you say if your child constantly grieves over being picked last for school teams and groups?

37. Is it inappropriate to children to see their parents naked at any age?

38. What are the chances that you will suffer from a diminished sex drive after having children?

39. If you could see into a crystal ball, and saw that as a result of having children you would never want to have sex again, would you still have children?

40. If your child died, would you allow his or her organs to be donated to save other children?

41. Do you believe in blood transfusions to save your child's life?

42. Would you send your child to boarding school? Why or why not?

43. At what age would you send your child to boarding school?

44. How will you instruct your children about the parts of their body that are private and should not be touched by other children or adults?

45. Do you feel that schoolteachers are always right?

46. Who will go to parent-teacher conferences?

47. Do you have the ability to tell a teacher he or she is wrong if you think so?

48. If a teacher says one thing about your child, and your child says another thing, whom do you believe?

49. How would you explain death to a child?

50. How would you explain to a child what happens to a person after death?

51. What would cause you to want your child to see a therapist?

52. If a child needs to see a therapist, is this a sign that the parent has failed or that the parent is enlightened?

Children have never been good at listening to their elders, but they have never failed to imitate them.

JAMES BALDWIN

IN *ESQUIRE*, 1960

53. If you take your child for therapy, would you re-linquish control to the therapist or insist that your approval be given for every strategy employed by the therapist?

54. Do you believe that teens as well as adults are the "creatures of circumstance" or the "creators of circumstance"?

55. If your teens discovered that you had been sexu-ally active or promiscuous before you got married, do you think they would then feel justified in replicating your behavior?

56. Should parents tell their children about past be-haviors they may not be proud of?

57. Would it bother you if your son wanted to be a ballet dancer? Why?

58. Would it bother you if your daughter wanted to be a boxer? Why?

59. What efforts will you make not to play favorites with your children?

60. Who gets to ride in the front seat, the oldest child or whoever gets there first?

61. To what lengths will you go to ensure that your children do not see you and your spouse making love?

62. What will you teach your children about masturbation?

63. What is the one thing your child could do that would disappoint you the most?

64. Should a teen who is more deserving get a better car than his or her sister?

65. What are the symptoms of a teen considering suicide?

66. If your teen is showing signs of considering suicide, what is the best way to approach the situation?

67. Is it appropriate for parents to comment negatively on their teen's hairstyle?

68. When a teen has pimples, should a parent volunteer how to treat them or wait to be asked?

69. What would you do if you discovered that your teen frequents porn Web sites?

70. When your teen is playing sports and a referee makes a call that you disagree with, what would your reaction be? What will your child learn from your reaction?

71. If your teen were called off to war and did not want to go, what would you do?

72. What would you do if you discovered that your son or daughter was taking steroids?

73. What would you do if your teen told you that your best friend just made a pass at him or her?

74. Would you consider your daughter's dress to be too short if the dress did not cover her knees when she sat down?

75. If you felt your daughter's dress was too short, what would you do about it?

76. Would you want your teen's temperament to resemble your own when you were a teen?

77. If your teen daughter wanted to take diet drugs to lose weight but had no real weight problem, what would you say or do?

78. How does a parent communicate the difference between love and infatuation to a teen?

79. How difficult will it be for you to value your teen's opinion, no matter how ridiculous it may seem?

80. If your teen asks for advice and you do not know the answer, should you say so or make something up?

81. What is good about children seeing that their parents are not afraid to cry?

82. Would you have a problem with your child dating someone of a different religion?

At every step the child should be allowed to meet the real experiences of life; the thorns should never be plucked from his roses.

ELLEN KEY, *THE CENTURY OF THE CHILD*

All happy families resemble one another; every unhappy family is unhappy in its own way.

TOLSTOY, *ANNA KARÉNINA*

83. What would you say to a child who wanted to marry outside of your religion?

84. Would you take out a second mortgage, leaving you financially strapped for the next thirty years, for an operation that gave your infant a 5 percent chance of survival?

85. Do you think that rape, incest, or the possible death of the mother are acceptable reasons for an abortion?

86. To what extent are parents to be held responsible for the actions of their children?

87. Are parents still responsible for the criminal acts of their adult children?

88. Think of the most valuable possession you own. How would you react if that possession were damaged or destroyed by your child?

89. What advice would you give to your child if he or she were being bullied in school?

90. How would you react if you learned that your child was the school bully?

91. If your child were in trouble with the law and were at risk of spending the next thirty days in jail, would you allow justice to take its course, or would you try to get your child out of trouble?

92. If you were on the brink of retirement, and your adult child needed to be bailed out of a gambling debt because he or she was at risk of physical harm, would you bail your child out even though you would have to push your retirement back two years?

93. Do you think you can ignore what the neighbors think about how you raise your children?

94. If you had a deceased parent with whom you had a bad relationship, would you share those bad memories with your own children? Why?

95. What effect would it have on your children if you cheated on their mother or father?

96. Do your children have a right not to want a relationship with you if you leave their mother or father?

97. What would you say to your married child who just confessed to having cheated on his or her own spouse?

98. What would you say to your married child whose spouse had just cheated on him or her?

Beyond the Couple

1. What kind of involvement do you want your parents to have or not have with your children?

2. What kind of relationship do you want your parents to have with your children?

3. When you think of each of your parents, who do you think has the best overall perspective and advice on raising an emotionally healthy family?

4. How would you feel about your family or friends administering discipline to your toddler, child, or teen?

5. Would you ask your family for money to help raise your children?

6. How often is too often to ask the same person to baby-sit?

7. Is it appropriate to ask someone to baby-sit while you go on vacation together?

8. Does your family get a say in your decision to adopt or not?

9. Does your family have a say on health issues for your child?

10. If you have family and friends who drop in all the time without notice to see the baby, would you be okay with that?

I should, many a good day, have blown my brains
out, but for the recollection that it would have
given pleasure to my mother-in-law; and, even
then if I could have been certain to haunt her ...

LORD BYRON

11. Do you have the ability to tell your mother, father, siblings, or friends to back off if they are giving you too many opinions or being critical of your parenting?

12. What would you say to your mother-in-law or father-in-law if either constantly made comments about your untidy home?

13. Who would you want to care for your children if you both died?

14. If you wanted another couple to take care of your children if you both died, should you seek the permission of the couple?

15. How much life insurance should you have on each of you for the benefit of your children?

16. In what ways have you judged your parents?

17. What issues have you judged your parents on that your own children could use against you as well?

18. If your teen reported to you that a teacher at school said she or he would fail in life, what would you do?

19. On what subject did you seek out the most advice from your parents?

Religion, Faith, and Ethics

1. What beliefs do you have about God that you want your children to have?

2. What religion, if any, will you encourage your children to participate in?

3. How would it affect you if your child wanted to embrace a different religion?

4. Why would God want or not want you to have children?

5. Have you ever had a spiritual revelation that you should have children?

6. How will you explain to your child why there are so many religions in the world?

7. What will you teach your child about the relationship between having a happy life and living the religion you choose for him or her?

8. What are the advantages of setting aside one night a week for the family to spend quality time together?

9. How do you define quality family time?

10. What will you teach your children about telling the truth?

11. Are there circumstances in your life in which you are not truthful and in which you would allow your children to be untruthful?

12. Is it wrong to bring children into a violent world?

13. How would you answer if your child asked you, "What is a soul? Do I have one?"

14. What values will you teach your children?

15. How will you teach values to your children?

16. Will you teach your children to pray? How often?

17. How will you explain to a child how God answers prayers?

18. Is it wrong to ask your children to live in a way that you are not living yourself?

19. If you and your spouse are of different religions but do not actively practice either, what happens when the time comes for a baptism, circumcision, or other religious ritual?

20. What will you teach your children about gambling?

21. Can organized religion have a negative impact on children?

22. How often will you attend religious services as a family, if at all?

23. If your primary reasons for having children are connected to your religious beliefs, what happens

Don't find fault, find a remedy.

HENRY FORD

There is nothing good or bad, but thinking makes it so.

WILLIAM SHAKESPEARE

If you could only love enough, you could be the most powerful person in the world.

EMMETT FOX

to your attitude toward your children if your religious views change completely?

24. If you raise your children in one religion their entire lives but later decide to change to another religion or abandon religion entirely, what effect will that have on your children?

 **Teenager Scenarios**

1. If you heard that your teen thought you were emotionally unavailable, what would you do about it?

2. To what extent is there a correlation between your teen's obedience to you and his or her overall happiness and success in life?

3. If your child turned out exactly like you, would that make you content? Why? Why not?

4. What effect do you think it has to constantly compare your children to each other?

5. If your teen daughter announced that she was pregnant, what would be your reaction? Would you allow her to live at your home? Should she get married? Would you help pay for her medical expenses?

6. To what extent do you feel that your children will "owe" you for having raised them?

7. Exactly what is it you feel they should owe you?

8. Describe your child as a teenager, according to the way you hope she or he will be.

9. How important is it to you to always know what is going on in your teenager's life?

10. What will you teach your teens about the limits of

The deepest principle in human nature is the craving to be appreciated.

William James

It is always easier to listen to unpleasant things after we have heard some praise of our good points.

Dale Carnegie, *How to Win Friends and Influence People*

physical contact between them and their boyfriends or girlfriends?

11. What would you say if your teen told you he or she was giving or receiving oral sex?

12. What would you do if you found out your teen was cheating in school?

13. What involvement should you have in the selection of your child's spouse? If your child's wedding day were today, what advice would you give?

14. At what point does a teen become obligated to contribute to the finances of the household, if at all?

15. Do you have plans for your child to learn a musical instrument?

16. If you felt that your teen should be the team captain, drama club president, or student body president but he or she were not selected, would you complain to the school about it?

17. Should teachers be made aware of your child's unique behavioral problems, or should they find out on their own?

18. How would you feel about your teen reading your journal?

It is the malady of our age that the young are so busy teaching us that they have no time left to learn.

ERIC HOFFER

No wise man ever wished to be younger.

JONATHAN SWIFT, *THOUGHTS ON VARIOUS SUBJECTS, MORAL AND DIVERTING*

19. Would you encourage your teen to keep a journal? Why?

20. Is there a time when it is appropriate or okay for just one child to go on a vacation or trip with just one parent?

21. When should children be given an allowance? How much? How often?

22. When should teens stop getting an allowance?

23. Should an allowance be given as a result of chores performed, or given without requirement?

24. Who will teach your children about sex?

25. At what age should children receive sex education from parents?

26. How do you feel about your child attending sex education classes at school?

27. How will you educate your children about drugs, alcohol, and sexual abuse?

28. How do you feel about home-schooling your children?

29. Will your children attend public or private schools?

30. To what extent are school grades a reliable predictor of success later in life?

It's frightening to think that when kids really want advice, they don't often enough go to the adults in their life, they go to their peer group.

RON TAFFEL, FAMILY THERAPIST

Some parents feel they've gotten through the "terrible twos" only to be confronted with the "terrible teens."

ANN LANDERS

31. What financial contribution should your children make to the costs of their education?

32. What limits will you place in your home on watching TV or playing video games?

33. At what point will you allow your children to make their own decisions without your interference?

34. How do you feel about being involved in your child's school activities, in parent organizations, in your child's youth groups, and so on?

35. What would you say to your teen if he or she wanted to drop out of high school or college to start a business?

36. Should teens be taught to work toward a career they love or toward one that will only pay well?

37. Should your teen have to be concerned about whether you approve of his or her career choice?

38. Would you prefer your teen to be an employer or an employee? Why?

39. Would you allow your teen to have his or her own computer, Internet access, or phone line?

40. Should a teen be allowed to lock the door to his or her room from the inside, from the outside, or not at all?

A depressed adult usually looks and feels sad and lethargic. A depressed teenager, on the other hand, may seem extremely angry and rebellious with "acting out" behavior such as school problems, truancy, sexual promiscuity, drinking, drug abuse, running away from home and other risk-taking problems.

KATHLEEN MCCOY,
COPING WITH KIDS WITH DEPRESSION

When parents refuse to consider any point of view other than their own, their teenagers tend to shut them out completely or confine conversation to unimportant issues.

Our teenagers don't expect approval for everything they do, but how can they develop faith in their own ideas if we continually overrule their decisions?

JAYNE NORMAN AND MYRON HARRIS,
THE PRIVATE LIFE OF THE AMERICAN TEENAGER

41. What will you do or say if your teen has a particular friend who you think is a bad influence?

42. What would you say or do if your teen came home with a tattoo, nose or nipple ring, or shaved head?

43. At what age will you allow your teen to pierce a body part?

44. At what age should your teen be allowed to date one-on-one?

45. What advice will you give to your teen before his or her first real date?

46. How do you feel about your teen choosing friends independently of what you think of the friends?

47. What type of relationship would you like to have with your teen?

48. In what ways will your relationship be different with a teenage son than with a teenage daughter?

49. What involvement should you have in your teen's choice of boyfriend or girlfriend?

50. What type of movies will you not allow your teen to watch?

51. Under what conditions would you allow your teen to drive your car?

Telling a person not to feel the way he feels does not take away the feelings. Disregarding your adolescent's true feelings makes him disregard you.

DOROTHY W. BARUCH,

HOW TO LIVE WITH YOUR TEENAGER

52. Who will help your teen with homework and how often?

53. At what age will you allow your teen to start working part time?

54. Under what conditions would you ask your child to pay room and board?

55. If your teen were in a school play that ran for five nights, would you go? How many times?

56. If your teen regularly competes in sports, who will go to cheer him or her on, and how often?

57. Would you cosign a loan for your teen's first car? Why or why not?

58. What should the curfew be for your teen?

59. Will your children have assigned chores in and outside the house? How will they be assigned?

60. How would you feel about your teenage daughter wearing a thong bikini?

61. If your teen were suspended from school for fighting, would you support the school's decision?

63. At what age do you think your child should be responsible for buying personal items such as clothes, shoes, CDs, DVDs, and the like?

64. How important is it that each teen in your family

have a first car that's approximately of the same value as the other's?

65. How do you know when your teen is overloaded with activities?

66. If your child is overloaded, what, if anything, should you do about it?

67. Is it okay for your teen to disagree with your opinions?

68. If your work causes you to travel a lot, would you take your teen with you when appropriate?

69. How would you feel about your teen becoming an exchange student in another country?

70. Do you think it would be more difficult to raise a teenage daughter or a teenage son?

71. At what age does it become acceptable for your daughter to wear makeup?

72. At what age does it become acceptable for your teen to go to rock concerts with friends?

73. What experiences did you go through in your own teenage years that will make you more empathetic toward your teen?

74. Do you think you should take it personally when your teen makes bad choices in life?

Some parents become hostile to the school or the therapist when their child shows unmistakable signs of improvement. This may be due to their resentment that someone other than themselves has succeeded where they have failed. The sad thing about such cases is that the child is removed from care at the highest point of dependence, thus tragically repeating the original trauma of deprivation.

ROBERT W. SHIELDS,
A CURE FOR DELINQUENTS

Don't complain about the snow on your neighbor's roof when your own doorstep is unclean.

CONFUCIUS

When dealing with people let us remember that we are not dealing with creatures of logic. We are dealing with creatures of emotion, creatures bristling with prejudices and motivated by pride and vanity.

DALE CARNEGIE, *HOW TO WIN FRIENDS AND INFLUENCE PEOPLE*

75. How does you stay detached from your teen's choices so that you don't take them personally?

76. If your teen repeatedly broke the curfew you had established, what would you do?

77. What would you say or do if your teen told you your schedule was too busy and that you needed to spend more time with the family?

78. What place does patience have in raising teenagers?

79. Would you allow your teen to ride a motorbike instead of or in addition to a car?

80. Is there an age at which parents are no longer responsible for their child's actions?

81. What would you do if you discovered that your teen had taken money from your wallet?

82. At what point do you tell your children that they need to live on their own?

83. If your teen commited an adult crime, should he or she do adult time in adult jail?

Impatience is the desire to have your needs met first. When your needs are taken care of, do you not then have patience with the needs of others?

GARY ZUKAV, *THE SEAT OF THE SOUL*

Conclusion

This is not a book of answers but a book of questions—issues you should consider before making the unbreakable commitment of having children. Of course there will be certain questions you don't know the answer to, but these answers are available by speaking to other people and reading specialized books. Many people say that parenthood has no manual to prepare would-be parents. Recognize this for what it is—a cliché and that's all. There are tons of manuals and books designed to aid the diligent parent, but too many offer only temporary solace. There is much I have to learn about pregnancy, parenthood, and the like, and you can bet your bottom dollar that my head will be immersed in books written by those who know more than I long after my wife announces she is pregnant.

So what can parents expect? To a very large extent, one could argue that the decision to have a child means

giving up any aspect of predictability in your life ever again. When it comes to parenthood, the only decision we have absolute control over is whether to have a baby or not. Pretty much all else is controlled by chance. Of course, we have some influence, but remember that influence is not control. A TV reporter interviewing me about my first book, *Don't You Dare Get Married Until You Read This*, said to me, "You are a man who doesn't like risks, aren't you?" His question was based on my comments about taking the unpredictability out of marriage by asking the right questions beforehand. However, when we decide to have children, we do not have the benefit of a prescreening interview—we cannot qualify our children. But I suspect that somehow the wisdom of the universe allows them to prequalify us. Good luck.

For Further Information

Corey Donaldson can be reached to answer questions, for comments, or for speaking availability at cphaid@aol.com.

DON'T YOU DARE GET

MARRIED

UNTIL YOU READ THIS!

THE BOOK OF QUESTIONS FOR COUPLES

Over 500 Points to Ponder
Before You Live Happily Ever After,
From Love and Sex to In-Laws,
Exes, and Dirty Laundry

COREY DONALDSON

Corey Donaldson helps couples get on the same
page about their plans, priorities, and life goals
before taking the big marital plunge in

DON'T YOU DARE GET MARRIED UNTIL YOU READ THIS!

0-609-80783-8

$12.00 paper (Canada: $18.00)

Available from Three Rivers Press wherever books are sold

THREE RIVERS PRESS • NEW YORK

www.randomhouse.com

Notes

Notes

Notes